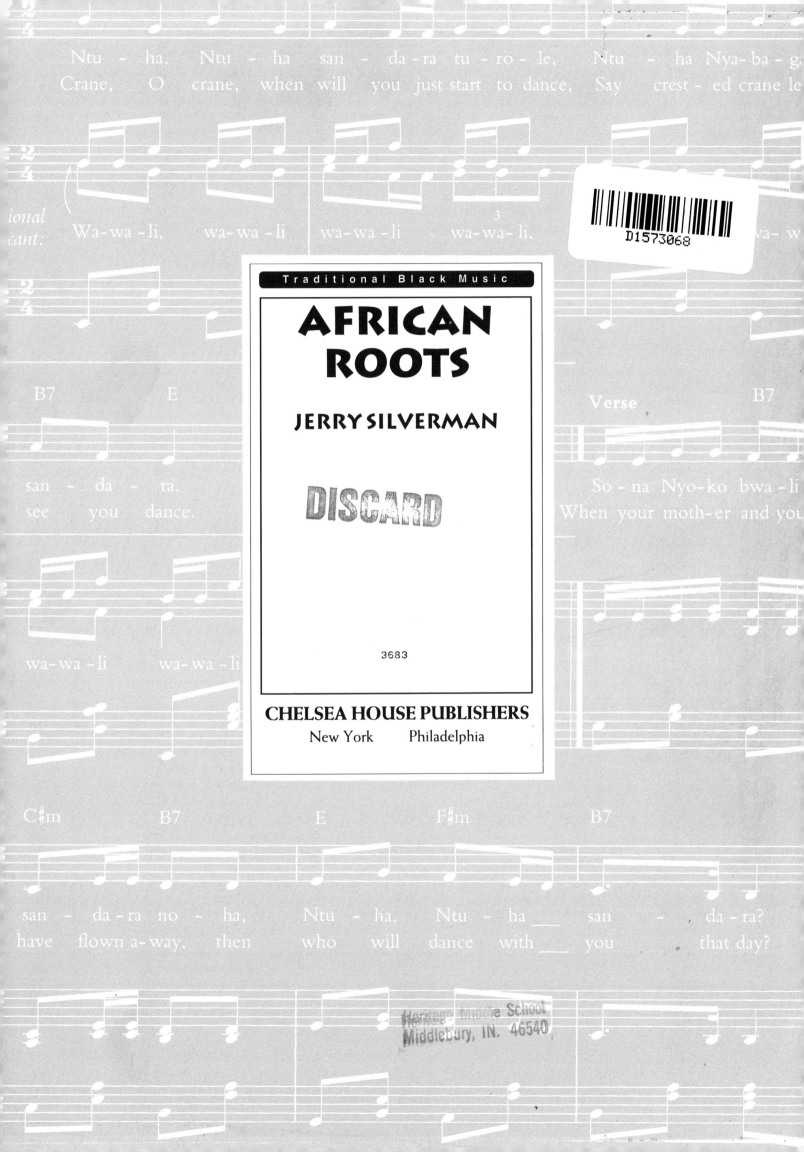

# AFRICAN ROOTS

Traditional Black Music

## JERRY SILVERMAN

DISCARD

3683

**CHELSEA HOUSE PUBLISHERS**

New York          Philadelphia

I would like to thank Mpho A. Tutu, director of the Bishop Desmond Tutu Southern African Scholarship Fund, for her invaluable assistance with a number of translations of song texts.

*On the cover* A xylophonist and two drummers play an ancient tribal song in the west African republic of Mali.

**Chelsea House Publishers**

Editorial Director  Richard Rennert
Executive Managing Editor  Karyn Gullen Browne
Executive Editor  Sean Dolan
Copy Chief  Robin James
Picture Editor  Adrian G. Allen
Art Director  Robert Mitchell
Manufacturing Director  Gerald Levine
Systems Manager  Lindsey Ottman
Production Coordinator  Marie Claire Cebrián-Ume

**Staff for African Roots**

Text Editor  Marian W. Taylor
Picture Researcher  Villette Harris
Book Layout  Jesse Cohen

First Printing
1  3  5  7  9  8  6  4  2

**Library of Congress Cataloging-in-Publication Data**
African roots / [compiled by] Jerry Silverman.
1 score. — (traditional black music)
For voice and piano: includes chord symbols.
English words.
Includes index.
   A songbook of African folk songs and music with pictures and captions.
0-7910-1828-8              0-7910-1844-X (pbk.)
1. Folk songs, English—Africa—Juvenile. 2. Folk music—Africa—
Juvenile. 3. Blacks—Africa—Music—Juvenile. [1. Folk songs,
English—Africa. 2. Folk music—Africa. 3. Blacks—Africa—Music.]
I. Silverman, Jerry. II. Series.                92-40384
M1830.A34 1993                          CIP  AC M

# CONTENTS

## Author's Preface

Sub-Saharan Africa's rich tapestry of traditional and contemporary music is closely interwoven with the lives of its people. From ancient hunting and ceremonial chants to the complex choral protest songs of today's social and political movements, this music has an immediacy that affects listeners and performers alike. And, as with folk music the world over, the line between audience and interpreter is often blurred.

In Africa's music, humor and pathos, subtlety and directness are blended in much the same fashion as they are in the songs of America's black population. Indeed, people on both sides of the Atlantic sing of life's troubles and joys with equal intensity. Consider a pair of examples: the African song "Manamolela" (Foreman) and the American "Told My Captain."

Manamolela, Manamolela,

Don't you see how tired we are,

Alas, we are so tired . . .

Captain, Captain, you must be blind,

Look at your watch, it's past quittin' time.

Captain, Captain, how can it be,

Whistle done blow, you still workin' me?

The roots of black American music can be easily traced eastward to their African origins (pentatonic scales, call-and-response chants, dance-driven rhythms), but in recent years the transatlantic flow has been running both ways. Saxophones, electric guitars, and synthesizers are now equally at home in black Africa and America. Songs such as "We Shall Overcome" and "Everybody Loves Saturday Night" have traveled not only across the ocean but around the world.

Melodic and appealing, the songs in this collection almost beg to be sung. In performing them, many of us will experience a kind of music totally new to us, but they offer even more than exciting sounds: a special insight into the culture of a people whose lives and aspirations are inextricably intertwined with our own.

Jerry Silverman

### The Contribution of Blacks to American Art and Culture

# Kenneth B. Clark

Historical and contemporary social inequalities have obscured the major contribution of American blacks to American culture. The historical reality of slavery and the combined racial isolation, segregation, and sustained educational inferiority have had deleterious effects. As related pervasive social problems determine and influence the art that any group can not only experience, but also, ironically, the extent to which they can eventually contribute to the society as a whole, this tenet is even more visible when assessing the contributions made by African Americans.

All aspects of the arts have been pursued by black Americans, but music provides a special insight into the persistent and inescapable social forces to which black Americans have been subjected. One can speculate that in their preslavery patterns of life in Africa, blacks used rhythm, melody, and lyrics to hold on to reality, hope, and the acceptance of life. Later, in America, music helped blacks endure the cruelties of slavery. Spirituals and gospel music provided a medium for both communion and communication. As the black experience in America became more complex, so too did black music, which has grown and ramified, dramatically affecting the development of American music in general. The result is that today, more than ever before, black music provides a powerful lens through which we may view the history of black Americans in a new and revealing way.

In Natal, the Zulu people's homeland in southeastern Africa, shoreline and interior landscapes offer a series of vivid contrasts. On the subtropical coastal belt, wild dates, ilalas, and wine palms bend and sway in the warm breezes from the Indian Ocean. In the interior uplands, westerly winds blow through dense forests of white ironwood and Cape beech trees, along with tracts of 150-foot-tall yellowwoods and other lofty evergreens. Higher still, the vast, grass-covered plateaus are punctuated only by an occasional windblown bitter karoo or thornbush. The birds that "rest when the trees do bend" include more than 1,000 species, ranging from the red-backed shrike and the white stork to eagles, kites, harriers, falcons, hawks, and owls.

# THE TREES BEND
## IMIT IGOBA GOSHLEH

Zulu

i – thi, Gu – nya – gaz a – ma shla – mvu, Go – nje, go – nje.
nice – ly, the leaves they are a stir – ring, stir – ring like this.

*Dancers in Zaire rustle and shake the tufts of grass they wear at wrist and ankle.*

For centuries, the outside world saw Africa as the Dark Continent, an almost unimaginably vast region teeming with danger and death, with deep mysteries and fantastic wealth. Here were fought wars of conquest and colonization; here was staged the 19th century's "Scramble for Africa"—the mad competition of European nations for the continent's gold, diamonds, ivory, and, of course, "black gold"—slaves. Africa's history has been traditionally recounted in terms of Europeans. But even as these foreigners invaded, explored, and plundered the continent, its own history was unfolding: native African empires were rising, gaining dominance, falling, and being reborn.

As the 20th century approached, Africans started turning their sights inward, rejecting and correcting the visions of a European-centered world. Now, in increasing numbers, Africans began to embrace their homeland with deeply felt nationalism and pride. It was in this spirit that schoolteacher Enoch Santanga, a member of South Africa's Xhosa people, wrote "Nkosi Sikel'i Afrika"——"Prayer for Africa"—in 1897.

# PRAYER FOR AFRICA
## NKOSI SIKEL'I AFRIKA

By Enoch Santanga

Xhosa

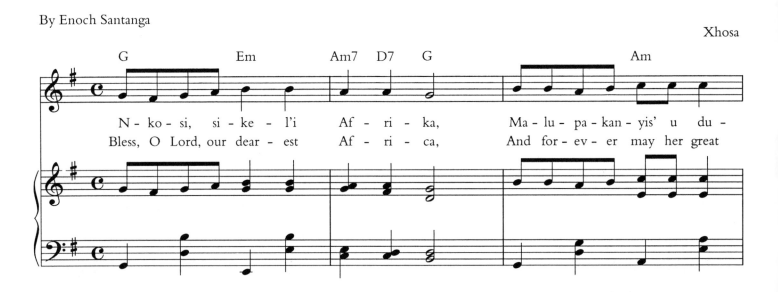

N - ko - si, si - ke - l'i Af - ri - ka, Ma - lu - pa - kan - yis' u du -
Bless, O Lord, our dear - est Af - ri - ca, And for - ev - er may her great

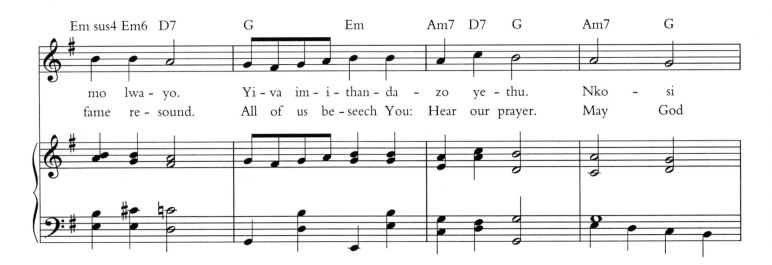

mo lwa - yo. Yi - va im - i - than - da - zo ye - thu. Nko - si
fame re - sound. All of us be - seech You: Hear our prayer. May God

In countries all over the world, the lion has always symbolized strength and majesty; in Africa, homeland of this "king of beasts," the lion is regarded with special respect—and fear. Shaka the Lion, the mighty Zulu conqueror of the 19th century, inspired just such reactions from his people.

Born about 1787, Shaka became chief of the Zulu clan—part of the Nguni group of the Bantu people—in 1816. He revolutionized the Zulu army, enlisted or exterminated his enemies, and conquered most of southern Africa, founding the Zulu Empire and ruling it with an iron hand until his death in 1828.

In this song, the locale where "the people are all finished" may change from verse to verse.

# HERE IS THE LION
## NANS'I NGONYAMA

Zulu

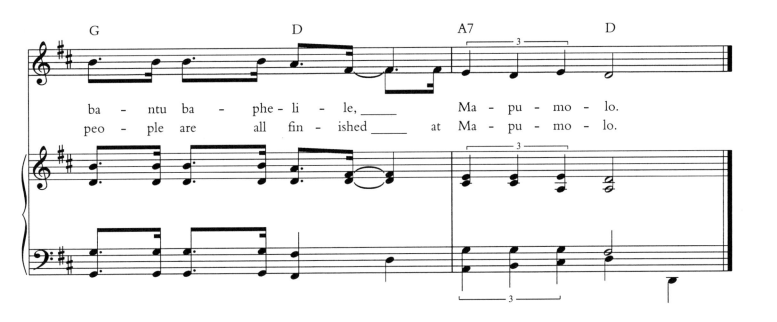

ba - ntu ba - phe - li - le, _____ Ma - pu - mo - lo.
peo - ple are all fin - ished _____ at Ma - pu - mo - lo.

Gathered around their campfire, the Zulu villagers anxiously await the hunters' return. Suddenly, an argument breaks out: Will the hunters bring back a lion (*ngonyama*) or a hippopotamus (*nvubu*)?

The earliest account of contact between Zulus and Europeans comes from survivors of the shipwrecked *Doddington*, a British vessel that sank off the southeastern coast of Africa in 1756. The Zulus, reported the British, were fastidious about personal cleanliness, extremely careful about the preparation of their food, and "very proud and haughty." That pride would become ever more evident. As the years passed and Europeans—most of them British or Dutch—began pouring into southern Africa, the Zulus were to rise up again and again, defending their territory with stunning skill and ferocity.

# LION, HIPPOPOTAMUS
## NGONYAMA NVUBU

Zulu

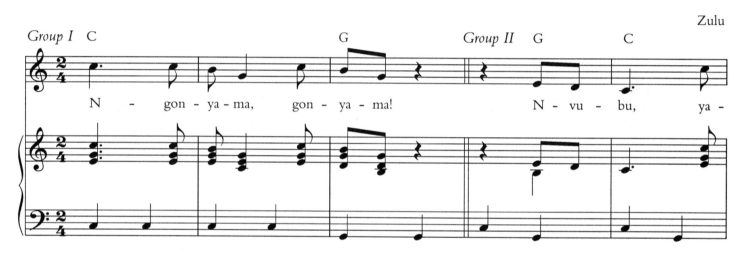

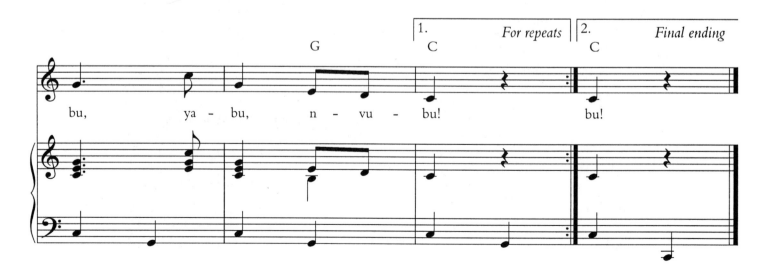

*Guinean drummers provide rhythmic accompaniment for a complex sacred ritual.*

"Guabi Guabi" is written in Fanagolo, a pidgin Zulu that enables workers—particularly miners—from different regions to communicate with each other. *Guabi Guabi*, which may be either someone's name or an untranslatable nonsense phrase, is a children's game. The first player, claiming that he is hiding a present or something good to eat, says to the second player, "Guess what I've got." He offers the second player a quick glance at the treasure, then hides it again. In this song, the singer is trying to make his girlfriend guess what he conceals—"tasty buns, sweets, or ripe bananas." (*Banana*, originally the Wolof word *banäna*, is the same in many languages, including English, Spanish, and Portuguese.)

# GUABI, GUABI

Zulu

Gua - bi, gua - bi gu ___ zwa - ngle nto - mbya - mi, I - hlal - e - nka-
Gua - bi, gua - bi, well ___ I have a girl - friend, She lives at Nka-

mben' shu - ngya - mta - nda, Gua - bi, gua - bi gu - nda. Ngi - za - mte-
mba, sure I love ___ her. Gua - bi, gua - bi, well _ - her. And I will _

nge - la ma - ba - nzi, I - zi - wi - chi, le ba - na - na, Ngi - za - mte-
buy for her tast - y buns and sweets __ and ripe ba - na - nas, Yes, I will _

nge - la - ma - ba - nzi, I - zi - wi___ chi le ba - na - na. ____
buy for her tas - ty buns and sweets_ and ripe ba - na - nas. ____

The Sutho people of southeastern Africa's plateau region have traditionally approved of marriage between cousins, accounting for the title of this humorous marriage song. Heard as far north as Nigeria, the tune is a three-quarter-time variant of a commercial that played incessantly on American radio stations in the 1940s: "I'm Chiquita Banana, and I've come to say / Bananas like to ripen in a special way . . ." Which came first, *Matsoala* or *Chiquita*? Who can say?

# HEY! COUSIN
## HEY! MATSOALA

Sutho

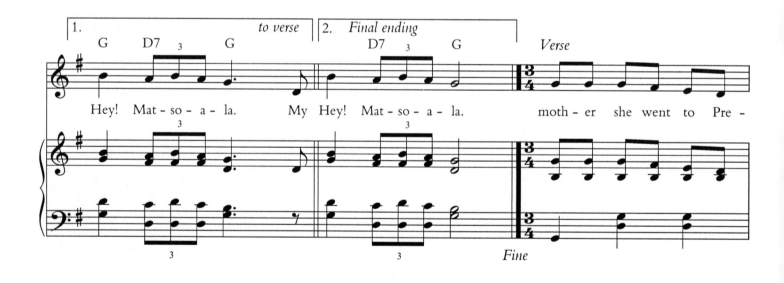

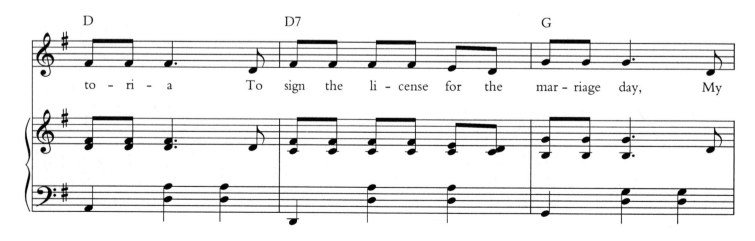

16

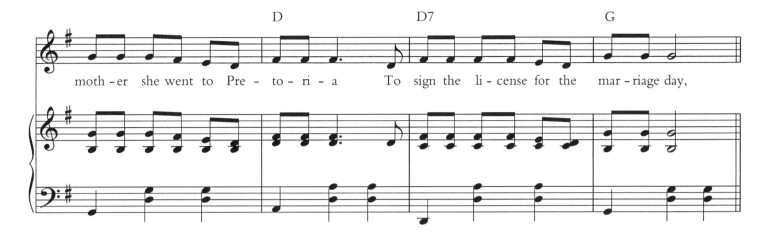

moth-er she went to Pre - to - ri - a    To sign the li - cense for the    mar - riage day,

My father, he will give the bride away.
He's just a-waiting for the dowery.
My father, he will give the bride away.
He's just a-waiting for the dowery. *(Chorus)*

*Apostolic church members sing hymns on a street corner in Brooklyn, New York.*

"Ko-ko-le-o-ko," an African version of the English rooster's "cock-a-doodle-doo," appears in this song from Liberia. A 43,000-square-mile nation (about the size of Tennessee) in southwestern West Africa, Liberia was founded in 1822 as a colony for freed slaves from the United States. Its establishment was inspired by the 19th century's Back-to-Africa Movement and funded by the Society for Colonizing the Free People of Color, a charitable organization sponsored by black and white Americans. Most of the world's major governments recognized Liberia as an independent nation in 1847, but it was not until 1862, in the middle of the Civil War, that President Abraham Lincoln extended U.S. recognition. English-speaking Liberia is now Africa's oldest black republic.

# THE ROOSTER'S CALL
## KOKOLEOKO

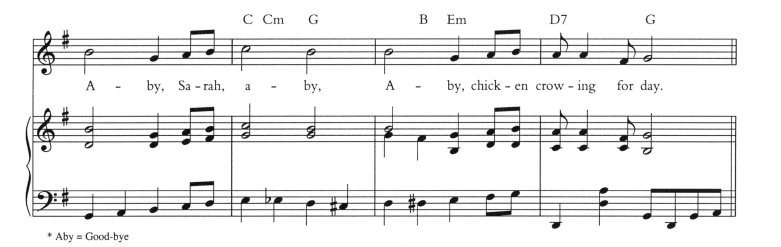

C  Cm  G          B  Em        D7        G

A - by, Sa - rah, a - by,    A - by, chick - en crow - ing for day.

* Aby = Good-bye

One more round, Tete, *
One more round.
One more round,
Chicken crowing for day. *(Chorus)*

Take your time, baby,
Take your time.
Take your time,
Chicken crowing for day. *(Chorus)*

* Tete is a girl's name.

The Liberian song "Come by Here" is well known in the United States as "Kumbaya"—a word that listeners will understand as soon as they hear or sing this variant.

# COME BY HERE

*Chorus*

As sung in Liberia

Come by here, ___ my Lord, come by here, ___ Come by here, ___ my Lord,

come by here, ___ Come by here, ___ my Lord, come by here, ___ O

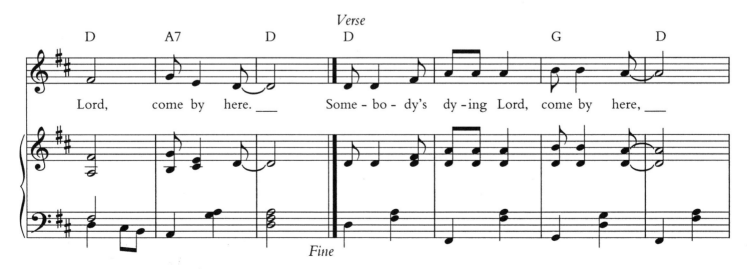

Lord, come by here. ___ Some-bo-dy's dy-ing Lord, come by here, ___

*Fine*

Somebody needs you, Lord,
Come by here.
Somebody needs you, Lord,
Come by here.
Somebody needs you, Lord,
Come by here —
O Lord, Come by here. *(Chorus)*

*Similarly*

Somebody's praying, Lord . . .

Somebody's weeping, Lord . . .

Somebody's calling, Lord . . .

Somebody's singing, Lord . . .

*Repeat first verse*

Africa's syncopated rhythms—splendidly demonstrated in this Liberian dance song—transplanted themselves to the New World, where they are now firmly rooted in West Indian calypso music. Much of black America's music, in fact, may be traced to the west coast of Africa, the area whose drumming became the motor force of American jazz.

# TAKE TIME IN LIFE

Liberia

I was pass - ing by, My broth - er called me in, And he

said to me, you bet - ter take time in life. Peo - ple, take time in life, Peo - ple

take time in life, Peo - ple take time in life 'cause you got far way to go.

I was passing by,
My uncle called me in,
And he said to me,
My nephew, take time in life.
    Nephew, take time in life,
    Nephew, take time in life,
    Nephew, take time in life,
    'Cause you got far way to go.

I was passing by,
Some people called me in,
And they said to me,
My young man, take time in life.
    Young man, take time in life,
    Young man, take time in life,
    Young man, take time in life,
    'Cause you got far way to go.

*Attired in the traditional robes of their West African nation, a Cameroonian flutist and drummer participate in a religious ceremony.*

A square dance, or quadrille, consists of a series of dance figures for four couples. In Liberia, the quadrille is performed to lively songs such as "I Goin' Chop Crab," in which the dancers—accompanied by gales of laughter—act out the movements described in each verse. A quadrille can last as long as the dancers' imagination can supply new verses. See how many you can make up and act out!

# I GOIN' CHOP CRAB

Liberia

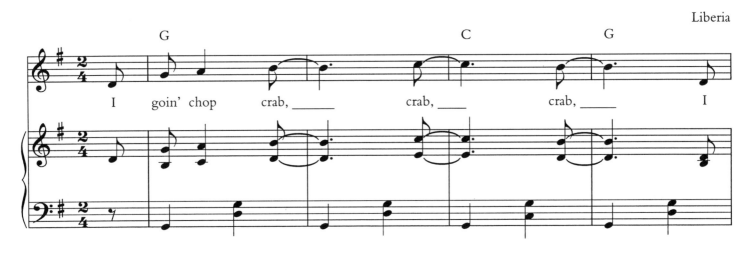

I'm goin' dig gold, gold, gold,
I'm goin' dig gold,
For me ma lover to live.

I'm goin' to plant farm, farm, farm,
I'm goin' to plant farm,
For me ma lover to eat.

I'm goin' to dig stone*, stone, stone,
I'm goin' to dig stone,
For me ma lover to sell.

I'm goin' to build house, house, house,
I'm goin' to build house,
For me ma lover to sleep.

I'm goin' to buy car, car, car,
I'm goin' to buy car,
For me ma lover to ride.

* stone = diamond

To do his job properly, the Xhosa witch doctor—a professional worker of magic who specializes in healing the sick—must be helped into the proper mood. This song is designed to do just that. Repeated over and over, it begins slowly and softly, then speeds up and becomes louder and more intense with every repetition. On the third beat of each measure, the word *bamba* is sung, at which point the singers slap their thighs. At the final *bamba*, the singers let out a breathless gasp. Literally, the words translate into English as "Ho, turn back around the hills, for we are going." For the best effect, however, sing the Xhosa words.

# HO! TURN BACK AROUND THE HILLS
## HO! JIKEL' EMAWENI

Xhosa

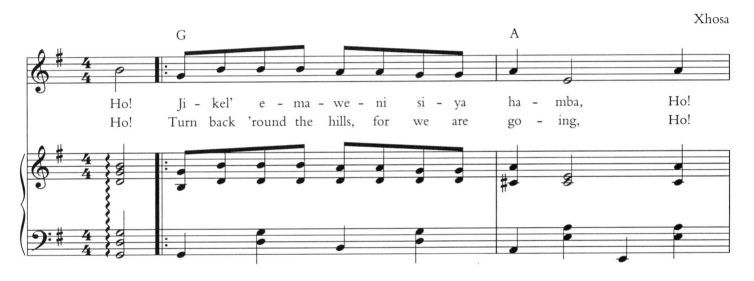

Ho! Ji - kel' e - ma - we - ni si - ya ha - mba, Ho!
Ho! Turn back 'round the hills, for we are go - ing, Ho!

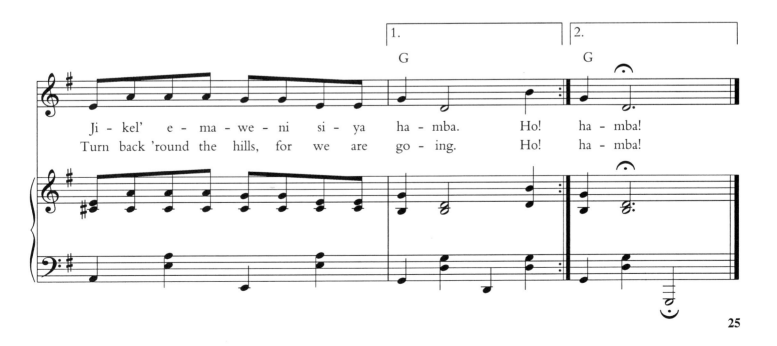

Ji - kel' e - ma - we - ni si - ya ha - mba. Ho! ha - mba!
Turn back 'round the hills, for we are go - ing. Ho! ha - mba!

Although most civil authorities officially forbid it, the ancient practice of buying a wife—in this case, giving the parents a dowry of "two goat, two cow, and sixteen sheep" in return for the bride—continues in many parts of the world. Nana Kru, the subject of this Liberian song, has only one choice: to depart with the man who has paid her dowry and claimed her for his wife.

# NANA KRU

Liberia

Na - na, Na - na Kru, Na - na, Na-na Na-na Kru,

Jump in - to my can - oe,____ Na - na I paid my dow-ry for

you. Na-na, Na-na -na -na Na - na, Na - na Kru, Na - na Kru,

Hoping to get a tasty snack, young people are inviting themselves into the home of their "dear teacher." This song comes from the Ugaba people of Ibadan, Nigeria.

# MAKE WE GO EAT
## KALO SILE

Nigeria

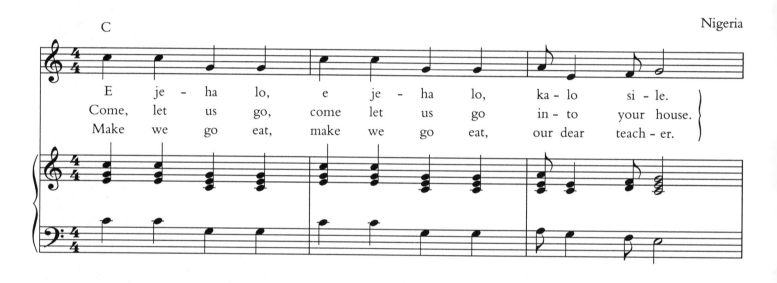

E je - ha lo, e je - ha lo, ka - lo si - le.
Come, let us go, come let us go in - to your house.
Make we go eat, make we go eat, our dear teach - er.

O!    O!    O!    O!

E je - ha lo ka - lo si - le.
Come, let us go, in - to your house.
Make we go eat, our dear teach - er.

*A worshiper in New York City celebrates the Oheneda Festival, an annual holiday observed by Ghana's Akan-speaking people.*

Here is another song born during the political rallies and demonstrations of Nigeria's midcentury march toward independence. "Everywhere There Must Be Freedom" is close in feeling to another great liberation song of the period: "We Shall Overcome," an old hymn and union song that became the anthem of the American civil rights movement.

# EVERYWHERE THERE MUST BE FREEDOM

*Chorus*

Nigeria

Free - dom, Free - dom, ev - 'ry - where there must be free - dom.

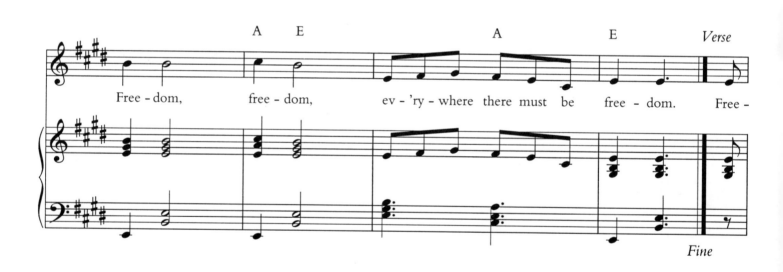

Free - dom, free - dom, ev - 'ry - where there must be free - dom. Free -

*Verse*

*Fine*

dom for you, __ free - dom for me, Ev - 'ry - where there must be free - dom, Free -

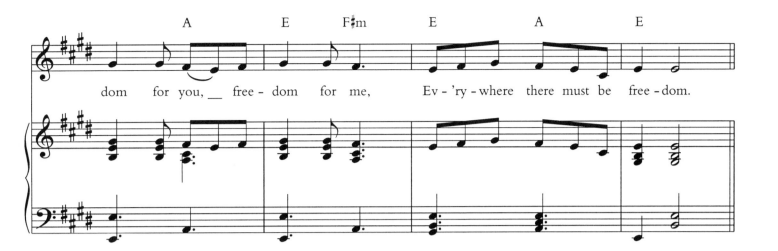

Freedom for one, freedom for all,
  Everywhere there must be freedom.
Freedom for one, freedom for all,
  Everywhere there must be freedom. *(Chorus)*

During the 1950s, British colonial authorities in Nigeria faced the serious challenge of a strong people's liberation movement. In a vain effort to suppress it, the officials imposed a six-day-a-week curfew; only on Saturdays did they allow the people to stage rallies and gather to sing, dance, and give speeches. "Bobo waro" grew out of those treasured Saturday nights. Over the years, the simple but exuberant phrase "Everybody loves Saturday night" has passed beyond Nigeria's borders and been translated into many languages.

# EVERYBODY LOVES SATURDAY NIGHT

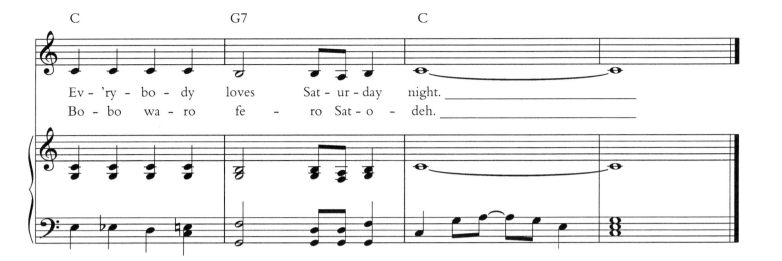

*Similarly*

*Chinese:* Ren ren si huan li pai lu . . .

*French:* Tout le monde aime Samedi soir . . .

*Ga:* Mofeh moni s'mo ho gbeke . . .

*Italian:* Tutti vogliono il sabato sera . . .

*Russian:* Vsiem nravitsa subbota vietcher . . .

*Spanish:* A todos les gusta la noche del sábado . . .

*Wolof:* Kouneke bougue neu gouidi Samdi . . .

*Yiddish:* Yeder eyner hot lieb shabas ba nacht . . .

*Yoruba:* Gbogo wale von Saturday . . .

"Asikatali," one of many songs to spring from Africa's black national liberation movement, came to the United States with Mary Louise Hooper, a San Franciscan who had spent several years in South Africa. Quickly adopted by America's civil rights movement, the song rang out over countless protests and demonstrations during the turbulent 1960s. In both Africa and America, freedom songs are often church hymns whose words have been adapted to fit current social and political needs.

# O, WE DON'T CARE
## ASIKATALI

South Africa

This Lutora-language song is from western Uganda. Its descant—a string of "wawalis" sung as a counterpoint to the melody—evokes the call of the African crowned crane, a tall wading bird famed for both its beauty and its powerful voice. Traditionally, sopranos deliver the descant.

# CRESTED CRANE
## NTUHA, NTUHA

Western Uganda

*D.C. al Fine*

Ebi soke ebi nyamwinyi,
Amajwenge g'e, Ntuha? *Chorus*

Tell me where you got that pretty crest.
That's the part I like the best.

*Chorus*

*A trio of white-robed Ghanaian women dance barefoot during a religious festival.*

In its sentimental lyrics and musical outline this Kenyan song will remind many readers of that perennial American favorite "You Are My Sunshine."

*You are my sunshine, my only sunshine,*
*You make me happy when skies are gray;*
*You'll never know, dear, how much I love you,*
*Please don't take my sunshine away.*

Is the resemblance coincidental? Probably not: before 1963, when Kenya gained its independence after more than a century of British rule, countless Kenyans must have heard "You Are My Sunshine" on records and at sing-alongs. Folk music often leaps national borders, adapting itself as it goes; America's "Sunshine" may have crossed the Atlantic Ocean and emerged as Kenya's "Tulipokuwa."

# WHEN WE WERE IN LOVE
## TULIPOKUWA TUKIPENDANA

Kenya

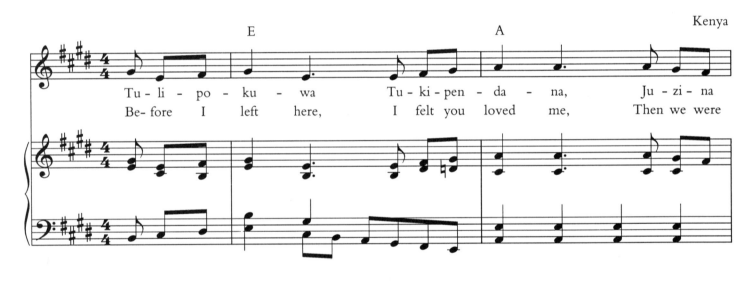

za - na, Ma- pen - zi ya - ko ni bu - re sa - na.
bad time, You were the near - est and dear - est to me.

| | |
|---|---|
| Mary ulidhani | Now since I've come back |
| Sitarudi tena | Once more to see you, |
| Kwenu mazera, | I hoped that we would |
| Ukatenda hayo | Be as before. |
| Nami kwa hakika | My heart's revealing |
| Sira haja rawe | You've changed your feeling, |
| Mapenzi yako | So I'll not come |
| Ni bure sano. | To your house anymore. |

This is a Bantu paddling song. Coordinating the paddling with the changing meters of this melody—whose downbeat keeps falling at different places—must make for some very interesting canoeing!

# O, Say to the Mother

## Sakola Nyango

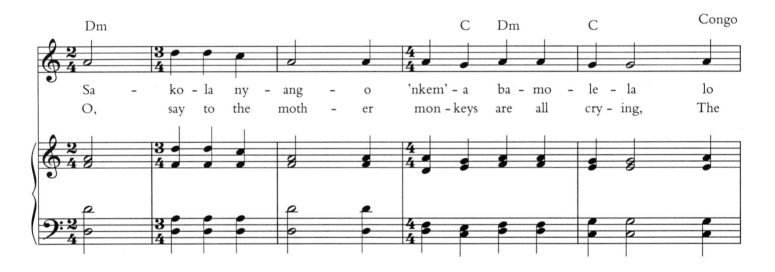

Sa - ko-la ny - ang - o 'nkem' - a ba - mo - le - la lo
O, say to the moth - er mon-keys are all cry - ing, The

mwa - no 'nkem' - a bu - ni lo ko-lo ba - mo - le - la.
lit - tle mon - key broke his leg, And they all are cry - ing.

*In New York's borough of Queens, Ghanaian immigrants practice an age-old ritual from their homeland.*

*The nomothotholos in the morning.*
*The nomothotholos are coming at dawn.*
*They're coming tomorrow, they're coming.*
*They're coming tomorrow, they're coming.*

Nomothotholos are mischievous spirits that hover over chimney tops, eavesdrop on conversations, and report interesting tidbits to the local witch doctor. Always up to something, these roguish creatures also steal; if they see any tobacco lying around, for example, they will dart down the chimney and seize it. You can conjure them up with this invocation—but be sure to sing it in the original Bantu; nomothotholos don't understand English!

# COME WITH THE DAWN
## BAYEZA KUSASA

*tacet chords*

Bantu

Oo-no-mo - t'ho-t'ho -lo, oo - no - mo- t'ho-t'ho - lo, oo - no-mo-

t'ho-t'ho -lo ba-ye- za, ku-sa - sa. Oo-no-mo - t'ho-t'ho- lo, ba-ye- za, ku

se – ni – na,       Oo –no –mo – t'ho –t'ho –lo  ba – ye–za,   ku – sa – sa.       Oo –no –mo–

t'ho–t'ho–lo.        Oo – no– mo –t'ho– t'ho –lo  ba – ye–za  ku–sa – sa  ba – ye – za.

Songs, hymns, and chants have always played a vital role in African nationalist meetings. American folk singer Pete Seeger learned this one from a tape recording brought to the United States in 1959 by Mary Louise Hooper, a San Franciscan who had spent several years in South Africa. Chief Albert Luthuli, the Nobel Prize–winning president of the African National Congress, identified "Tina Sizwe" as one of his special favorites. It is another fine example of the choral-singing genre.

# TINA SIZWE

South Africa

46

Abantwana, abantwana beh Afrika bakalela, bakalela, i Afrika
Elatatwa, elatatwa, abamhlo,
Mabonyehe, mabonye, kumhlaba, we,
Mabonyeke, mabonye, kumhlaba, wetu.

We, children of Africa are crying for Africa
That was taken by the white people.
They must leave our land alone!
They must leave our land alone!

After toiling all day in the broiling sun, farmhands plaintively appeal to their *manamolela* (foreman): "Alas," they sing, "we are so tired!" Americans can find echoes of this Sutho work song and the feelings that inspire it in countless black ballads from their own working world. "Told My Captain" is one of them:

*Captain, Captain, you must be blind,*
*Look at your watch, it's past quittin' time.*
*Captain, Captain, how can it be,*
*Whistle done blow, you still workin' me?*

# MANAMOLELA

Sutho

The lullaby is probably the most universal of all songs. This one, from South Africa, is sung in Bantu—a group of more than 500 languages spoken in central and southern Africa—but its gentle sound would probably soothe any baby in the world.

# SOFTLY, SOFTLY
## T'HOLA, T'HOLA

Bantu

T'ho - la, t'ho - la ngoa - na - me; T'ho - la, t'ho - la, ngoa - na - me,
Soft - ly, soft - ly, my ba - by; Soft - ly, soft - ly, my ba - by.

Li pe - re se - ra peng. _____ Ra - peng sa - ma ha - pu.
Hush, it is just the wind _____ Blow - ing through the branch - es.

Ei - tsa li lo tse - la tsa ea - ngoa - na - me, E pu - tsoa ea khao - ha mo
Once on a time was a young li - on ba - by, Took him to the doc - tor to

Choral singing plays a major role in traditional Bantu music, in which interlocking contrapuntal lines and lilting voices combine to produce beautiful sound. Boys sing "Somagwaza" at their manhood-initiation ceremony. As the young men are receiving instruction about the duties and responsibilities of adult citizenship, they live apart from the rest of the village. During this time, the teachers daub their students with ceremonial clay. When the training is over, the boys—now officially men—race down to the river to wash, singing "Somagwaza" as they go. This song's words, like those of many ceremonial chants, have lost their exact meanings, but their effectiveness remains. It is felt rather than understood.

# SOMAGWAZA

Bantu

52

Bantu parents sometimes tell their children bedtime stories that feature the fearsome monster Abiyoyo.  The little ones love Abiyoyo tales, but they sometimes need a bit of calming down after a particularly scary one; on such occasions, parents croon this gentle lullaby.  Enthralled by hearing his name sung, Abiyoyo forgets his evil intentions and begins to dance.  Before long, he falls asleep, exhausted—and so do the children.  Pete Seeger has recorded the story and song, and the author has many times lulled his own children to sleep with it.

# ABIYOYO

Bantu

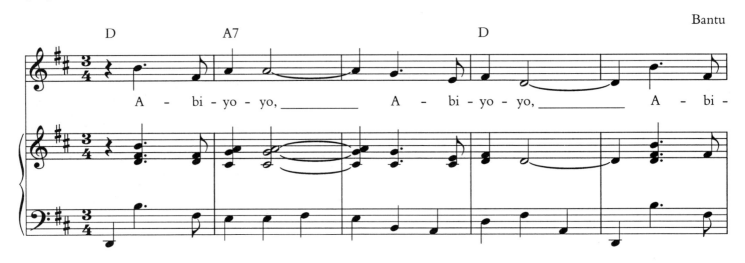

A - bi - yo - yo, _____ A - bi - yo - yo, _____ A - bi -

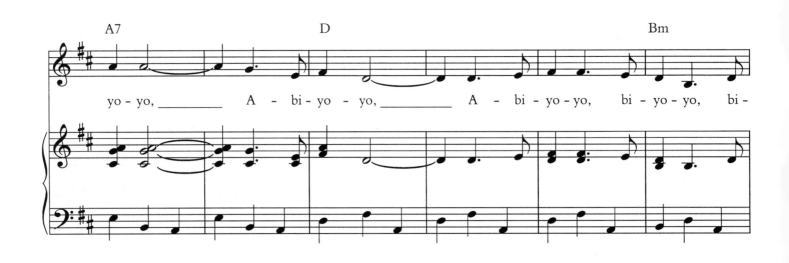

yo - yo, _____ A - bi - yo - yo, _____ A - bi - yo - yo, bi - yo - yo, bi -

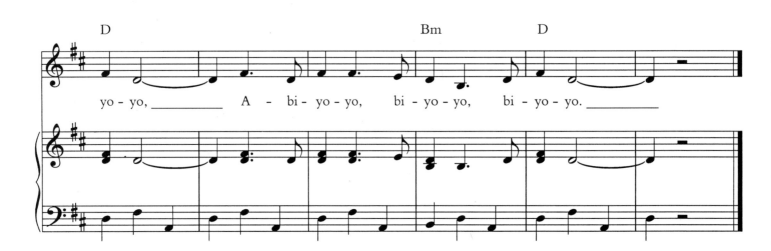

yo - yo, _____ A - bi - yo - yo, bi - yo - yo, bi - yo - yo. _____

*Honoring their African forebears, black Americans celebrate an ancient Yoruba Orisha rite in New York City's Harlem.*

This song, in the Mandingo language of Gambia, involves three elements: the kernel of the oil palm tree, source of palm wine; Janke Wale, onetime king of the Kabu region of Guinea Bissau; and Janke Wale's son, Tura Sane. The people of Gambia gather to drink palm wine and sing "Cewe Lenkele Wecho," accompanying themselves on the *kora*, a guitarlike instrument with a gourd for a resonator.

# THE OIL PALM KERNEL
## CEWE LENKELE WECHO

Gambia

Mue, Jan- ke Wa — le, Ce- we len- ke - le we- cho, ce we len- ke - le. Ten-
Hear, Jan- ke Wa — le, The o - il palm tree ker- nel, the o - il palm tree. The

ku - lu kum- ba we- cho, ce- we len - ke - le we- cho, ce- we len - ke - le. Tu -
ker- nel of the oil palm, the o - il palm tree ker - nel, the o - il palm tree. Tu -

ra Sa — ne le, Ce- we len - ke - le we- cho, ce- we len - ke - le. Ten-
ra Sa — ne o, The o - il palm tree ker - nel, the o - il palm tree. The

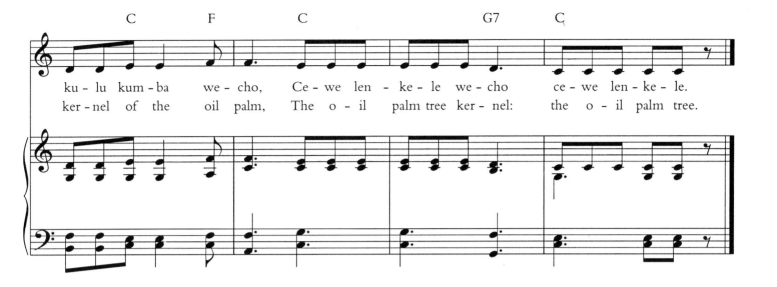

ku - lu kum - ba we - cho, Ce - we len - ke - le we - cho ce - we len - ke - le.
ker - nel of the oil palm, The o - il palm tree ker - nel: the o - il palm tree.

Ghanaian students sing this charmingly simple song in honor of their mothers.

# MY DEAR MAMA
## KÉBÉ MAMA

Ghana

Ma - ma, ké - bé Ma - ma, O, ké - bé Ma.
Ma - ma, my dear Ma - ma, O, my dear Ma.

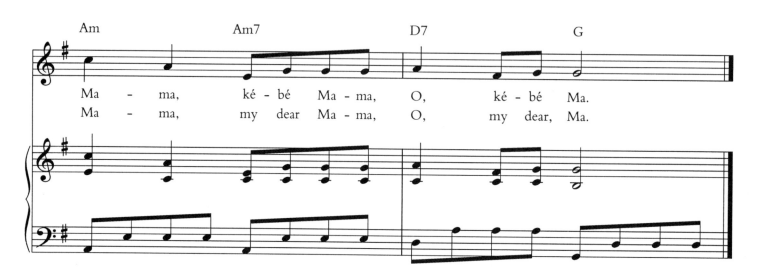

Ma - ma, ké - bé Ma - ma, O, ké - bé Ma.
Ma - ma, my dear Ma - ma, O, my dear, Ma.

*Members of a Ghanaian choral society, the Azizanya Singing Band, await their cue at an open-air concert.*

American educator Edna Smith Edet, who served as head of the music department at the University of Nigeria in N'Sukka from 1960 to 1967, learned this traditional song and story from her Ibo students. Although each student told the story in his or her own distinctive regional dialect, the basic story—about a mistreated orphan boy and a magic fruit—was always the same. (The song's recurring "n-da" is a rhythmic interjection.)

The story is about a little boy called Chinyere. His mother was dead, and he was forced to live with his cruel stepmother. One day she gave her own son some udala (a fruit similar to a juicy peach), but she refused to give any to Chinyere. He begged his stepbrother for a bite, but the brother just spat a seed at him and ran away laughing. The hungry little boy put the seed in his mouth, but there was no fruit left on it, and he began to cry. With that, his mother rose up and told him to plant the seed on her grave and then to sing a special song: "Udala'm." The seed quickly grew into a very tall tree, and from then on, whenever Chinyere sang his song, the tree would bend its branches and pick him up so he could gather fruit. The tree always refused to let the cruel stepmother or her mean son pick a single fruit, but Chinyere never went hungry again, and he grew up to be rich and happy.

# UDALA'M

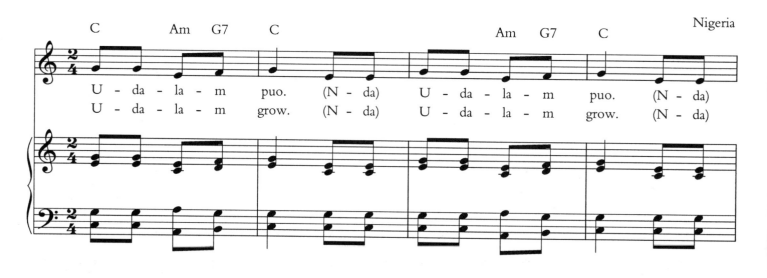

**Song and story from The Griot Sings, by Edna Smith Edet (Medgar Evers College Press, 1978). English translation of the lyrics by Edna Smith Edet. Used by permission of the author.**

Once upon a time there lived a little boy named Chinyere. He was very sad and unhappy. His mother had died, and he was forced to live with his father's second wife. His stepmother gave him very little to eat and physically abused him whenever she could.

One day the stepmother went to the market and bought some udala. When she returned home she gave the fruit to her own children. Chinyere had not eaten for two days, so he begged his little brother for some of the fruit. The brother said, "You want my udala? You want some of my fruit? Here you dirty thing, eat this!" With that, the brother spit the seed out of his mouth to the ground and ran away laughing.

Chinyere was almost in tears. Imagine how his younger brother had talked to him, the firstborn of the family. But he could do nothing, for what a child says he has heard at home. He picked up the seed to see if there was any fruit on it and seeing none, he began to cry bitterly. He cried until his mother rose up from the grave asking, "What has happened to my son?"

Chinyere told his mother of his unhappy life. She told him to plant the seed on her grave and to be sure to tend it and water it daily. She also taught him the song he had to sing to get his tree to grow in two days.

Chinyere planted the seed and then he started to sing, "Udala'm puo puo puo puo . . ." After he sang the song, the seed germinated, and you could see the stalk sticking out of the ground. Even though he was still hungry, he was happy. He knew he would have his own udala'm tree.

The next day he came to see the plant, and lo and behold, it had grown some more. So he sang "Udala'm to" and the tree grew tall, "Udala'm Mis" and the tree began to bear fruit, "Udala'm cha cha" and the fruits ripened.

From then on, when he wanted to eat he would sing his song and the tree would bend down to pick him up to pluck fruits.

His brothers and sisters grew envious and begged him for some udala, but he refused. They ran crying to their mother to tell her what had happened. She told her eldest son to hide and listen when Chinyere went to pluck his fruit. The young boy learned the song and one day he went and sang "Udala'm . . ." The tree bent down so that he could climb, but when it found out that it had been tricked it stood erect and stranded the boy up in the tree.

The other children ran to get their mother. The mother and her children begged the tree to bend down. They tried to pull the tree down, but it was no use. The mother looked around for an ax, but couldn't find one. Finally they sent for Chinyere to command the tree to let go, saying pleadingly, "Relatives should help each other so no one will hurt them." Chinyere scoffed at them, saying, "Relatives? Is that what I am now? You did not remember me before. I will not help you now."

The stepmother, seeing that Chinyere was adamant, called the father, who ordered him to free his brother. Chinyere said, "My younger brothers have not given me respect. Now that my mother is dead, you have forgotten you have an older son. I will not set my brother free."

This was the ultimate insult. An African child respects his elders and does not talk back to his father. The father decided to report Chinyere to the elders of the town.

When the elders came, Chinyere's father and stepmother excitedly began to tell the story. When they got to the part where Chinyere refused to let his brother down from the tree, the elders stopped them and turned to Chinyere and said, "Let your brother down, we command you."

Chinyere was perplexed. He knew he would have to obey the elders, yet he knew his cause was just. So he said, "You see my clothes, they are ragged and worn. Is this the clothing of the eldest son? You see my bones, I am starved for food. Is this what should happen to the eldest son? You see my bad behavior. It is because I am starved for affection and trust. Is this the way an eldest son should act? You are the chiefs of the town and I will do what you say. But if this is the way that life is to be lived in Ibo land, I no longer need my life." With this Chinyere turned around and called to the tree to let his brother down.

The elders had been shaking their heads during the story. They went to the side and conferred. When they returned they said to the parents, "You no longer have an eldest son. We will take from you all that is rightfully his, one half of what you own. Since you do not appreciate your eldest son we will give him to a family who will appreciate him."

They did all that they promised, and Chinyere went to live elsewhere. Since he was now rich and happy, he did not have to depend on the udala tree for food. But every couple of days he would return to his mother's grave so that the udala tree could hold him in its branches.

*Covered by a huge umbrella and accompanied by musicians, an Ashanti chief takes part in a formal procession in Ghana.*

## Index to Titles

## Index to first lines

**Jerry Silverman** is one of America's most prolific authors of music books. He has a B.S. degree in music from the City College of New York and an M.A. in musicology from New York University. He has authored some 100 books dealing with various aspects of guitar, banjo, violin, and fiddle technique, as well as numerous songbooks and arrangements for other instruments. He teaches guitar and music to children and adults and performs in folk-song concerts before audiences of all ages.

**Kenneth B. Clark** received a Ph.D. in social psychology from Columbia University and is the author of numerous books and articles on race and education. His books include *Prejudice and Your Child*, *Dark Ghetto*, and *Pathos of Power*. Long noted as an authority on segregation in schools, his work was cited by the U.S. Supreme Court in its decision in the historic *Brown v. Board of Education of Topeka* case in 1954. Dr. Clark, Distinguished Professor of Psychology Emeritus at the City University of New York, is the president of Kenneth B. Clark & Associates, a consulting firm specializing in personnel matters, race relations, and affirmative action programs.